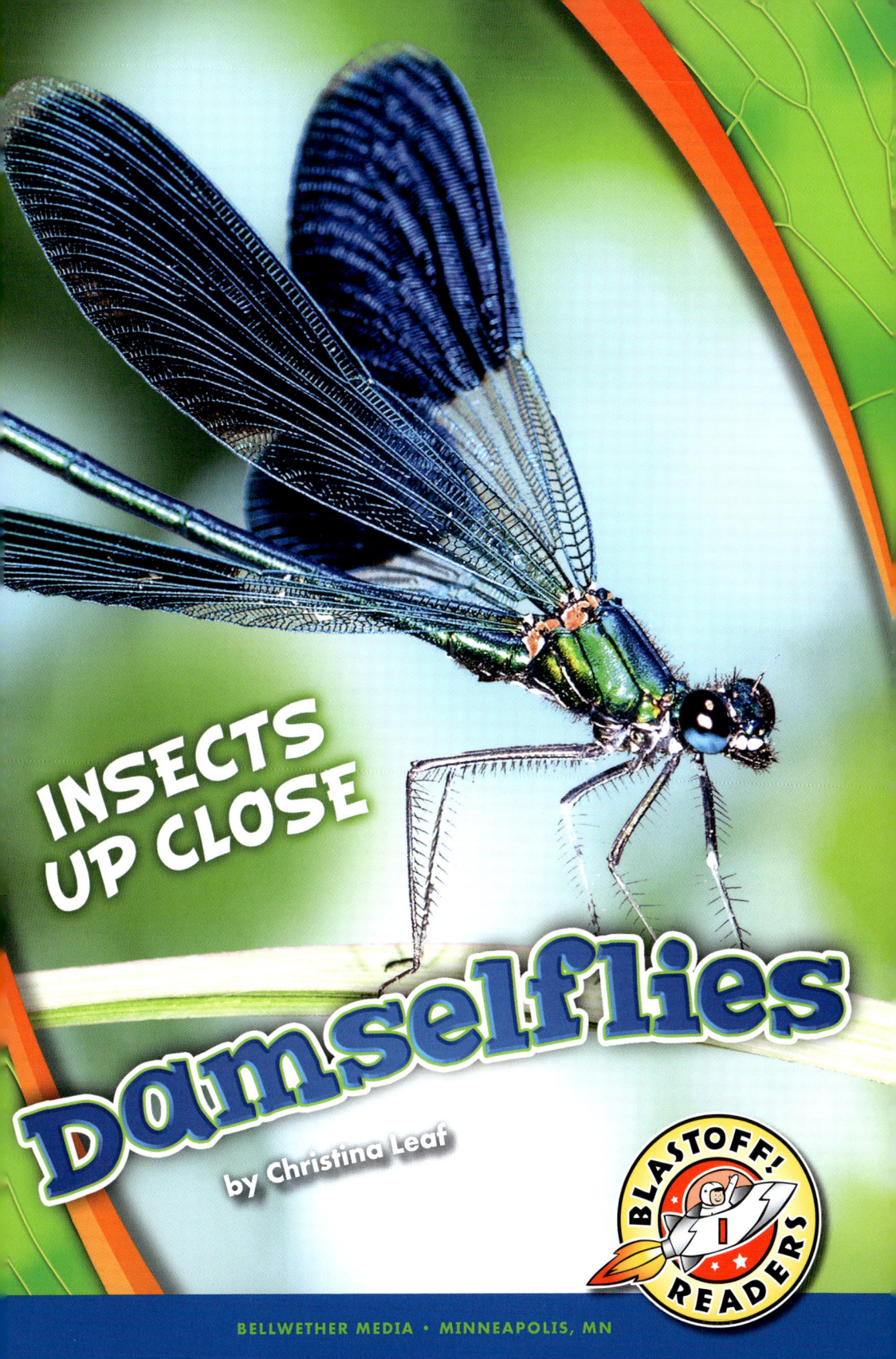

INSECTS UP CLOSE

Damselflies

by Christina Leaf

BLASTOFF! READERS

BELLWETHER MEDIA • MINNEAPOLIS, MN

Note to Librarians, Teachers, and Parents:

Blastoff! Readers are carefully developed by literacy experts and combine standards-based content with developmentally appropriate text.

Level 1 provides the most support through repetition of high-frequency words, light text, predictable sentence patterns, and strong visual support.

Level 2 offers early readers a bit more challenge through varied simple sentences, increased text load, and less repetition of high-frequency words.

Level 3 advances early-fluent readers toward fluency through increased text and concept load, less reliance on visuals, longer sentences, and more literary language.

Level 4 builds reading stamina by providing more text per page, increased use of punctuation, greater variation in sentence patterns, and increasingly challenging vocabulary.

Level 5 encourages children to move from "learning to read" to "reading to learn" by providing even more text, varied writing styles, and less familiar topics.

Whichever book is right for your reader, Blastoff! Readers are the perfect books to build confidence and encourage a love of reading that will last a lifetime!

This edition first published in 2018 by Bellwether Media, Inc.

No part of this publication may be reproduced in whole or in part without written permission of the publisher. For information regarding permission, write to Bellwether Media, Inc., Attention: Permissions Department, 5357 Penn Avenue South, Minneapolis, MN 55419.

Library of Congress Cataloging-in-Publication Data
Names: Leaf, Christina.
Title: Damselflies / by Christina Leaf.
Description: Minneapolis, MN : Bellwether Media, Inc., 2018. | Series: Blastoff! Readers. Insects Up Close | Audience: Ages 5-8. | Audience: K to grade 3. | Includes bibliographical references and index.
Identifiers: LCCN 2016055081 (print) | LCCN 2017004926 (ebook) | ISBN 9781626176614 (hardcover : alk. paper) | ISBN 9781681033914 (ebook)
Subjects: LCSH: Damselflies–Juvenile literature.
Classification: LCC QL520 .L43 2018 (print) | LCC QL520 (ebook) | DDC 595.7/33–dc23
LC record available at https://lccn.loc.gov/2016055081

Text copyright © 2018 by Bellwether Media, Inc. BLASTOFF! READERS and associated logos are trademarks and/or registered trademarks of Bellwether Media, Inc. SCHOLASTIC, CHILDREN'S PRESS, and associated logos are trademarks and/or registered trademarks of Scholastic Inc.

Editor: Christina Leighton   Designer: Maggie Rosier

Printed in the United States of America, North Mankato, MN.

Table of Contents

What Are Damselflies?	4
By the Water	10
Growing Up	16
Glossary	22
To Learn More	23
Index	24

What Are Damselflies?

Damselflies are insects with large wings. They hold their wings together to rest.

Damselflies have long, thin **abdomens**. Their colorful bodies often shine in sunlight.

ACTUAL SIZE:
blue-fronted dancer

abdomen

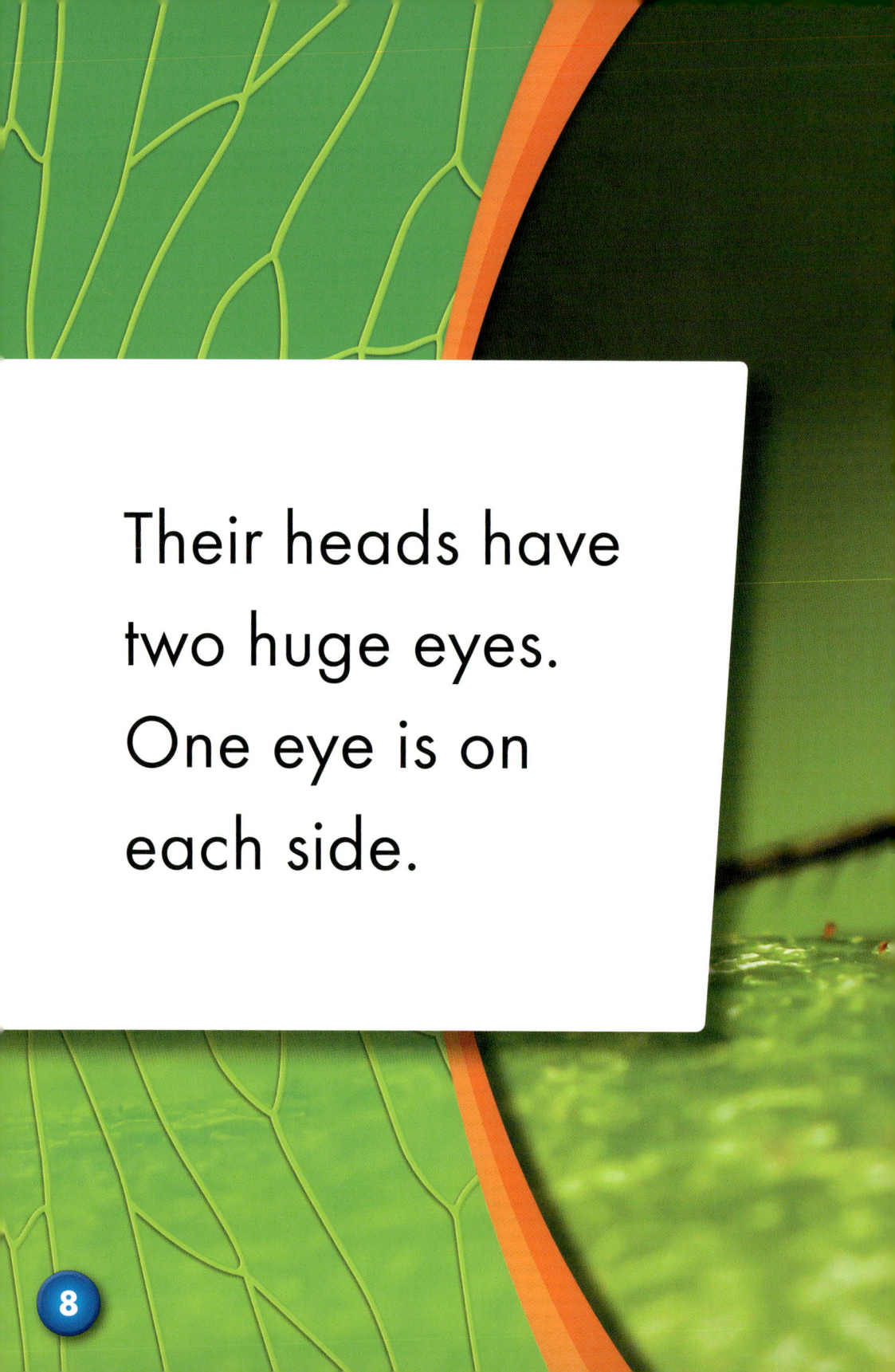

Their heads have two huge eyes. One eye is on each side.

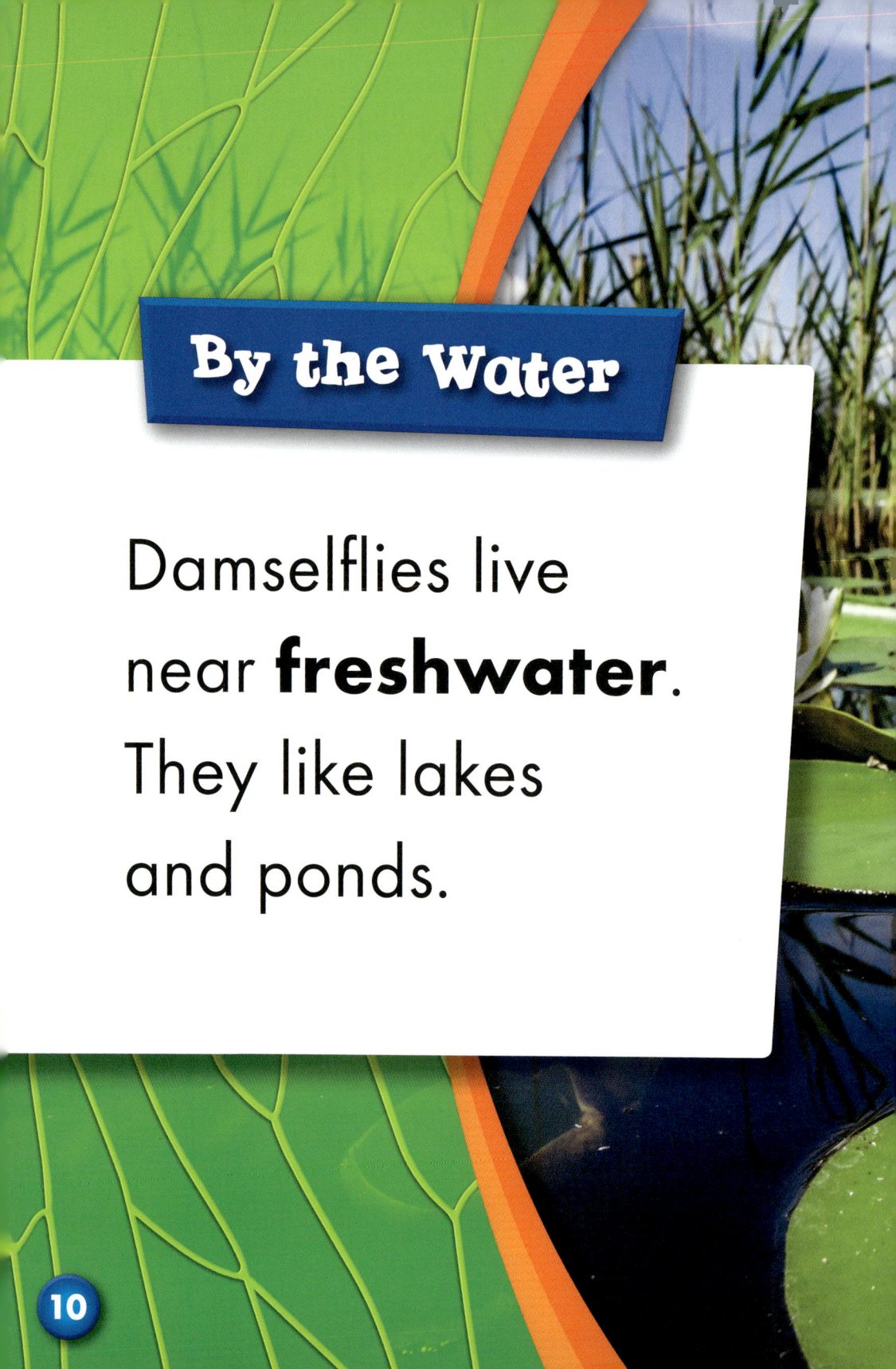

By the Water

Damselflies live near **freshwater**. They like lakes and ponds.

freshwater

Damselflies often rest in the sun. They must warm their wings to fly.

Damselflies are **predators**. They catch other insects in the air!

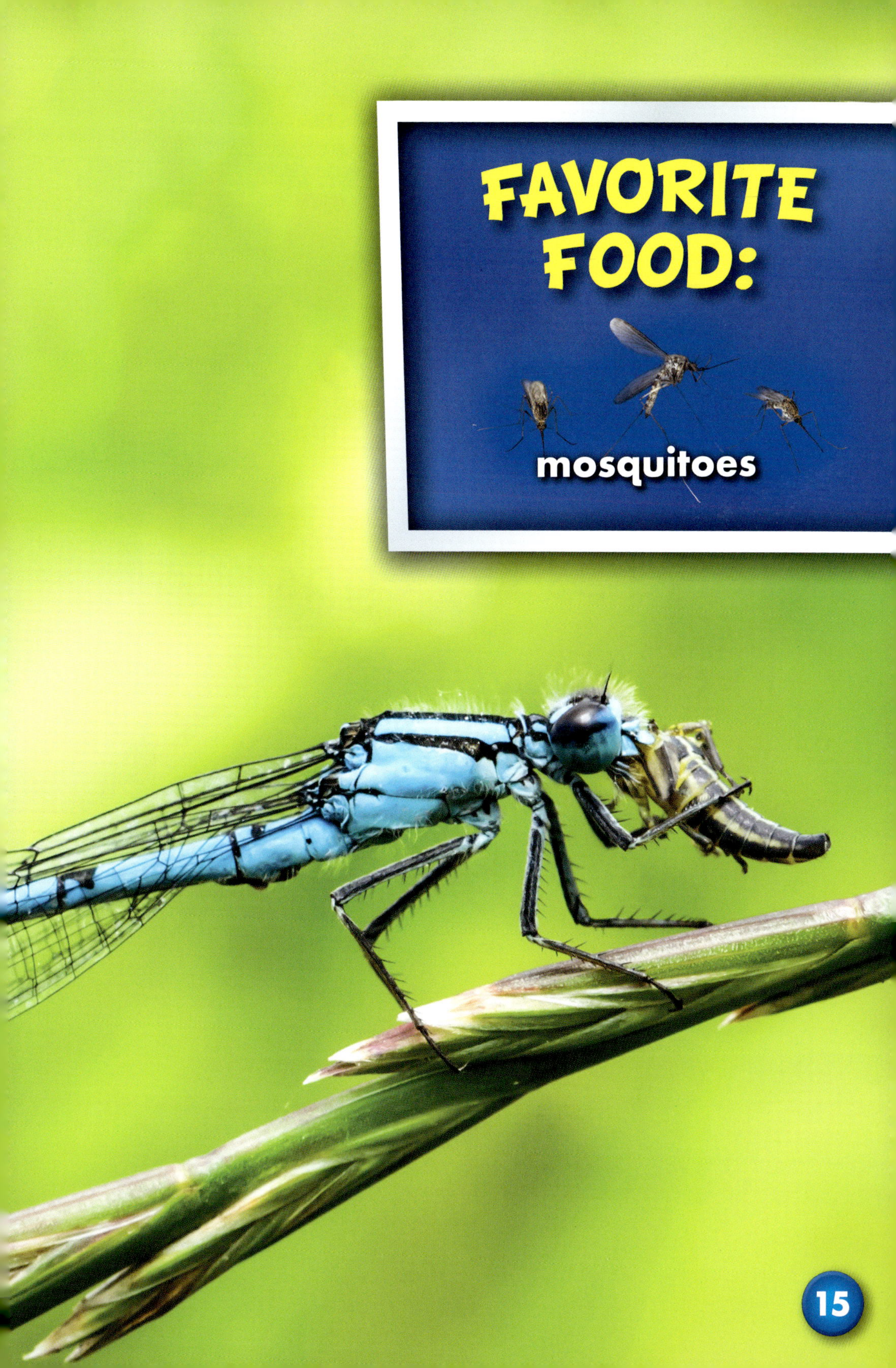

FAVORITE FOOD:

mosquitoes

Growing Up

Females lay eggs in or by water. They put the eggs in plant **stems**.

DAMSELFLY LIFE SPAN:
1 to 2 years

female laying eggs

Baby damselflies come from eggs. The **nymphs** live in water. They **molt** to grow.

Then the nymphs climb onto land. They molt one last time. Stretch those wings!

Glossary

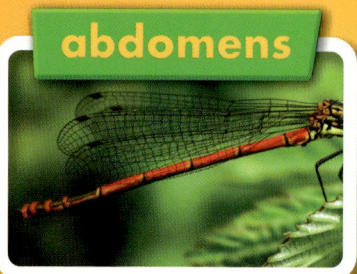

abdomens — the back parts of insect bodies

nymphs — young insects; nymphs look like small adults without full wings.

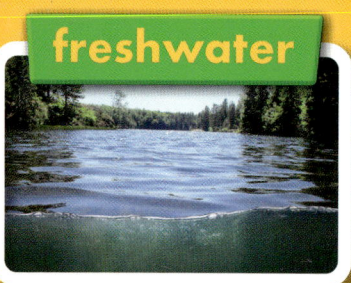

freshwater — water that is not salty

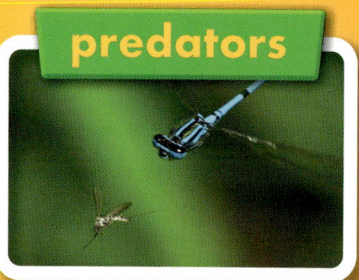

predators — animals that hunt other animals for food

molt — to shed skin for growth

stems — the long body parts of some plants

To Learn More

AT THE LIBRARY

Hughes, Catherine D. *Little Kid's First Big Book of Bugs.* Washington, D.C.: National Geographic Society, 2014.

Murawski, Darlyne, and Nancy Honovich. *Ultimate Bug-opedia: The Most Complete Bug Reference Ever.* Washington, D.C.: National Geographic, 2013.

Perish, Patrick. *Dragonflies.* Minneapolis, Minn.: Bellwether Media, 2018.

ON THE WEB

Learning more about damselflies is as easy as 1, 2, 3.

1. Go to www.factsurfer.com.

2. Enter "damselflies" into the search box.

3. Click the "Surf" button and you will see a list of related web sites.

With factsurfer.com, finding more information is just a click away.

Index

abdomens, 6, 7
air, 14
bodies, 6
eggs, 16, 17, 18
eyes, 8, 9
females, 16, 17
food, 15
freshwater, 10, 11
heads, 8
lakes, 10
land, 20
life span, 17
molt, 18, 20, 21

nymphs, 18, 19, 20
ponds, 10
predators, 14
rest, 4, 12
size, 7
stems, 16
sunlight, 6, 12
water, 16, 18
wings, 4, 5, 12, 20

The images in this book are reproduced through the courtesy of: MBadnjar, front cover; Mirko Graul, pp. 4-5; fotogaby, pp. 6-7; Amanda Blom Photography, pp. 8-9; Alex Huizinga/ NIS/ Minden Pictures/ SuperStock, pp. 10-11; yanikap, pp. 12-13; G.Moon, pp. 14-15; Willi Rolfes/ age fotostock, pp. 16-17; Stephen Dalton/ Minden Pictures/ SuperStock, pp. 18-19, 22 (top right); IamTK, pp. 20-21, 22 (bottom left); Mark Carthy, p. 22 (top left); Avesun, p. 22 (center left); Jausa, p. 22 (center right damselfly); Henrik Larsson, p. 22 (center right mosquito); Aleoks, p. 22 (bottom right).